Course Correcting –

Crafting an Operating Strategy that Fits You!

from

6 Steps to Getting Your Business on Track to Success

by

Thomas C. Browne

Published by

GrowthUS Associates, LLC

North Andover, MA USA

2014

Preface

I just returned from a flight over New England. The colors are rich in red and gold, the sky is clear, the air is crisp. Autumn is in its glory, a sure sign that people are plotting their strategy for next year!

I've found that being aloft gives you clarity looking ahead. It's not prescience, just presence. The advantage of being there.

Crafting an Operating Strategy that Fits You! is intended to help you craft your strategy in a form that lasts as well as succeeds. You can read a myriad of books on strategy; they tell you what worked for someone else or what you should do based on someone's theory but they rarely give you the framework for developing a strategy that springs from the well *within* you, that fits the world *around* you and yet reflects the wisdom of people who have *been* you and succeeded.

In the overall book of which this is a chapter, I've drawn on the experiences of a host of people who have been in *exactly* your position in order to help you plot your course from that position to where you really want to go. Other chapters will help you choose your destination, determine the best course to get there, help you stay on track and get you there quicker!

Throughout the book, you'll see a liberal sprinkling of hyperlinks. You can read the book and get a lot of insights without ever clicking a hyperlink but if you want to find an even richer trove of information, click the links and they will take you to places I doubt you'd ever see on your own!

Stories, back stories, amazing biographies, useful toolkits and astute guidance that I've assembled in my search for answers to the questions that I know you have, because I've had them too. But I didn't want to limit what you would get from this book to what you would get from *my* experiences alone so I added two dimensions which I hope you'll find helpful:

1. I'll save you a ton of time Googling to find answers.

Just hit the links and *"I'll Take You There!"* as the song goes.

2. I've interviewed a rich cross-section of people who've been there too.

I call this group The Delphi Council and they are profiled in the section by that name. Their comments have informed and shaped this book, their quotes are right on point, their stories are themselves very interesting and I've included links to where you can learn more about them. The book has also been shaped by my Editor, whose unique profile is included as well.

Their contribution to this book has been invaluable and I am profoundly grateful to them.

I hope the insights of the collective group of people who've contributed to this book will give you presence, if not prescience, as you navigate the twists and turns of your own path to Success!

Thomas C. Browne
North Andover, MA USA
October 2014

The Author

Thomas C. Browne, President, GrowthUS Associates, LLC

T. C. Browne is a successful operating executive experienced in venture, corporate and military environments as well as a serial change agent motivated by achieving breakthrough results.

As Chief Executive Officer & President of five high-tech venture companies as well as Senior Vice President & General Manager with BBN Corporation / GTE and Vice President, Corporate & Government Marketing with Sony Electronics, Inc., Mr. Browne has built the teams and shaped the strategies required to develop and deliver innovative products and services spanning Internet / wireless & satellite networks, computer software, contract R&D services, hosted applications solutions, network security & control, audio/video products and inertial microelectronics systems for multi-national business and defense customers on five continents.

As varied as all these technologies and as diverse as all the customers, they turn out to be *not* all that different in the needs they have, how the value of solving them gets measured and what it takes to align the motivations of all the people involved toward addressing the common goals.

A combat-veteran US Navy pilot and humanistic enterprise leader, TC brings his business and technology innovation experience to bear as he helps companies break new ground to build and transform their businesses. He has captured many of the tools he has used along the way and drawn on the insights of practical as well as academic experts in the field to share with others in his book *Course Correcting – 6 Steps to Getting Your Business On Track for Success!*

Mr. Browne earned a Bachelor of Science in Physics from The College of William & Mary in Virginia and a Master of Science in Administration with a concentration in Management Science and Operations Research from The George Washington University.

The Editor

David Sollars, President, David Sollars Consulting

David Sollars has entertained, educated, and inspired audiences with his experiences in personal and organizational development for more than 25 years. He shares these insights and guides audiences to discover their full potential through his efforts as a keynote speaker, workshop facilitator, non-profit chairman of the board, coach and consultant to corporate leaders. David has developed a curious mind set, which he developed as a serial entrepreneur having achieved success within the industries of media, manufacturing and medicine.

His extensive experience in design and delivery of executive education includes academic affiliations from Harvard Medical School, MIT Sloan School of Management, The International Consortium for Executive Development Research and Merrimack College, with industry leaders such as Unilever Global, Otsuka Pharmaceutical Company, Lundbeck Pharmaceutical, Bank of America Merrill Lynch, South Street Strategy Group, Heineken USA, AstraZeneca, Honda of America, Parker Hannafin and Philips International. David brings a diverse world of experiences in assisting individuals and top teams discover practical solutions through developing their own personal high performance habits.

David is a published author and contributor to numerous books and peer-reviewed journal articles. He is a senior editor for the nation's leading evidence-based research database in the emerging field of integrative medicine and is a frequent contributor and diplomat for the American Institute for Stress.

David is a Certified John Maxwell speaker, trainer and coach. He is an Executive Coach with Harvard Business School's Advanced Management Program (AMP) and a member of the coaching cadre at MIT's Executive Education Department. He holds a Master's degree from The New England School of Acupuncture and a BFA from the Actors Studio Program at Wright State University.

The Delphi Council

Chuck Auster, Managing Partner, Auster Capital Partners

Chuck Auster has more than 30 years of experience creating value through entrepreneurship, large corporate executive management, and private equity investments and transactions. Before establishing ACP, Chuck was a Partner and Managing Director at One Equity Partners ("OEP"), the private equity arm of JPMorgan Chase.

Among other transactions, Chuck led the deal team in the acquisition of Polaroid Corporation by OEP and served as Chairman of the Board of Polaroid.

Prior to joining OEP, Chuck spent 8+ years operating within the telecom and technology industry growing and taking companies public. He acted as President and CEO and was a Member of the Board of Directors of Info crossing, Inc. (NASDAQ:IFOX), a premier provider of a full range of IT outsourcing services, including mainframe and open systems, as well as complex hosting and managed services.

Chuck was also a Founder, and formerly the Executive Vice President and Chief Operating Officer and a Member of the Board of Directors of IXnet, Ltd. (Nasdaq:EXNT), a network provider of communication services offering an international voice and data for the financial services community. He was in a leadership role as part of the senior team that negotiated the sale of IPC and IXnet to Global Crossing in a stock-for-stock exchange valued in excess of $3.8 billion.

Chuck graduated from Tufts University with Highest Honors in Economics and holds a JD with Honors from the National Law Center, George Washington University. He is a member of the District of Columbia Bar and the Virginia State Bar.

David N. Campbell, Founder & Chairman, All Hands Volunteers, Inc.

David Campbell was until recently Executive Director of All Hands Volunteers, Inc., a not-for-profit volunteer-based disaster response organization he spontaneously created in January of 2005 in response to the devastating tsunami that wiped out coastal areas of Thailand. All Hands subsequently staged volunteer relief efforts in response to Hurricanes Sandy and Katrina, floods in Iowa and natural disasters in Haiti, Bangladesh, Peru, Philippines and Indonesia, always achieving maximum impact with minimum bureaucracy. In recognition of this significant humanitarian accomplishment, David was recently awarded the Encore.org Purpose Prize.

David was previously Managing Director of Innovation Advisors, a strategic advisory firm in the information technology software and services industry which he founded in November 2001. He served as President and Chief Executive Officer of Xpedior, a provider of information technology solutions, from 1999 to 2000 and previously, as President of the GTE Technology Organization from 1997 to 1999. From 1995 to 1999, David was President of BBN Technologies, a unit of BBN Corporation that was acquired by GTE Corporation. From 1983 until 1994 he served as Chairman of the Board and Chief Executive Officer of Computer Task Group, Incorporated.

David was appointed by President Clinton to the Advisory Board of the President's Commission on Critical Infrastructure Protection. During the past five years, in addition to leading All Hands, David served on the Board of Directors of Tektronix Inc. (prior to its acquisition by Danaher Corporation) and has served as a Director of Gibraltar Industries, Inc. since the Company's initial public offering in 1993, a post which he will leave on December 31, 2014.

Mr. Campbell holds Bachelor of Science degree from Niagara University and a Master of Science degree from State University of New York at Buffalo.

Jim Furneaux, President, Furneaux & Co., LLC and Founder, Kodiak Venture Partners

James H. (Jim) Furneaux's forty-year high tech career has spanned investment banking, venture investing and direct entrepreneurship. He was heavily involved in building businesses that commercialized a variety of semiconductor, personal computer, wireless and related technologies. As an investment banker, he helped structure transactions that raised billions of dollars in capital for companies which became industry leaders, including Intel, Applied Materials and Scientific Atlanta as well as category pioneers such as Telenet, the harbinger of Internet technology.

As an operating executive he led Spectra Inc., which pioneered hot-melt printhead technology that enabled convenience color printing, founded and led Chrysalis Symbolic Design which pioneered formal verification tools for semiconductor design and organized and was Chairman of Aironet Wireless Communications, which became a key WiFi platform for Cisco Systems, Inc.

As a venture investor at LF Rothschild Unterberg Towbin, Bessemer Venture Partners and later Furneaux & Company, he invested in early stages at Apple, Compaq Computer, Bright Horizons, Aironet Wireless and others. He co-founded Kodiak Venture Partners with his son Dave and has remained an active angel investor in recent years.

Jim is a 1966 graduate of Northeastern University, served from 1967 to 1972 as a US Air Force officer in the NRO satellite program and earned an MBA in 1974 from Dartmouth's Amos Tuck School of Business Administration.

Dr. Vlatka Hlupic, Professor of Business and Management, University of Westminster and CEO, Drucker Society London

Dr. Vlatka Hlupic is a Professor of Business and Management, Director of the Emergent Leadership and Development research group and Director of the Executive Coaching and Leadership Development Programme at Westminster Business School, a former Adjunct Faculty Member at London Business School and the Founder and CEO of the Drucker Society London, set up to help young unemployed people achieve their aspirations.

She received a PhD in Information Systems at the London School of Economics, as well as Dipl Econ. and an MSc in Information Systems from the University of Zagreb. She has published over 150 articles in journals (including Harvard Business Review), books and conference proceedings mainly in the area of leadership, knowledge management, business process change and business process modelling. Vlatka is an associate editor, a guest editor and a member of Editorial Boards for a number of international journals.

She has multi-disciplinary interests and is a Chartered Engineer, European Engineer, Fellow of the British Computer Society and Operational Research Society as well as a Certified Master Coach, Licensed Master NLP Practitioner, and Psychological Kinesiology Practitioner.

She is a renowned Leadership and Change Management Consultant and has advised major international organizations including the House of Commons, GlaxoSmithKline, BP, NHS, LearnDirect, Brand Velocity USA, the Drucker Institute USA and the Croatian Government.

Click here for more information about Dr. Hlupic, her work and her latest book.

Steven Koltai, Managing Director, Koltai & Company, LLC

Steven Koltai is the Managing Director of Koltai and Company, LLC (KoltCo), a professional services consulting firm that designs, implements, and advises on entrepreneurship ecosystem programming in emerging markets.

Steven created and ran the Global Entrepreneurship Program for Secretary of State Hillary Clinton, a central element of President Obama's strategy for changing the relationship between the U.S. and Muslim communities around the world. He left the State Department to continue the work of global entrepreneurship ecosystem building via Koltai & Company. Steven is currently a Guest Scholar at the Brookings Institution. Steven has over 30 years of business experience with several successful startups under his belt, including SES, the world's largest commercial TV satellite system, and Event411, an online event management business which he founded, grew to over 250 employees, and sold in 2002. He has also served as Senior Vice President for Strategy and Corporate Development at Warner Bros., as a strategic planning consultant at McKinsey & Co., and as an investment banker at Salomon Bros. Steven is an active angel investor and mentor to entrepreneurs around the world.

Steven holds a B.A. degree from Tufts University as well as an M.A. from Tufts Fletcher School of Law and Diplomacy, where he was a Fulbright Scholar.

Scott Maxwell, Founder & Senior Managing Director, OpenView Partners

Scott has been a Venture Capitalist since 2000, first as a senior Managing Director at Insight Venture Partners and then as the founder of OpenView Venture Partners.

At OpenView, and previously at Insight, Scott worked to develop and communicate the vision that an institutionalized venture capital firm can — and should — offer meaningful value beyond the capital that it invests. He has spent over a decade iterating on that approach, which includes the development of OpenView's investment focus and team, the OpenView Labs team, and the firm's content sites for executives.

Prior to becoming a Venture Capitalist in 2000, Scott spent the 1990s primarily working with financial services companies. He was a Partner at Putnam Investments, where he was Managing Director, Corporate Development, and was appointed to run Putnam's alternative asset management program. Previous to Putnam Investments, he was a Senior Vice President at Lehman Brothers, where he was the Chief Financial Officer of the Global Equity Division and a member of the Global Equities Executive Committee. Before Lehman, he was a management consultant at McKinsey & Company, where he focused primarily on financial institutions.

Scott spent the 1980s as a technology designer and developer, and was responsible for designing and developing automation systems at two California-based start-up companies. During that time, he also lectured at California State University, Sacramento.

Scott graduated from MIT with a doctorate degree in mechanical engineering and a master's degree in management from the Sloan MBA program. He also has a bachelor's degree and a master's degree in mechanical engineering from the University of California, Davis.

Tom Miller, President & Founder, T.R. Miller Co., Inc.

Founded in 1975 by Tom Miller, T.R. Miller Co., Inc. has grown from a one-man start-up to become an industry leader, ranking in the top 5% of the $20 billion recognition and promotional products industry and serving over 5,000 customers worldwide. Based in Walpole, Mass., T.R. Miller successfully promotes their clients' businesses with quality custom-branded merchandise, corporate recognition programs and company-store loyalty programs.

Tom's enduring personal values have guided the growth of his company as it focuses on building value for its customers' brands, in the process building an industry reputation for quality products, innovative ideas, reliable service, prompt delivery dates... and extremely fair prices.

Tom studied Marketing and Management at both Bentley University and Boston University while playing amateur league hockey before taking time out to help out with the family business. Serendipitously, he ended up creating a *new* one that has been recognized by the Family Business Association as their Northeastern success story!

The Process

The creation of this book leveraged the power of the Internet (an "impersonal network") as well as the strength of a personal network in a process that coupled research as well as one-on-one interviews to broadly develop useful content around the central theme of *Course Correcting*.

Whether you're an aviator, a mariner or a landlubber, you know that to get from A to B, you need to first determine the relative positions of A and B and then set a course that will get you to your destination. Along the way, you'll get pushed off that course, in which case you'll need to correct your course to either get back on your original track or plot a new course to point B.

Business is just like that except more complex since it involves so many forces which can push you off course, the unpredictability of what B will be like when you get there and the dynamics of the human dimension that is inherent in dealing with people.

This book is part of a journey of its own, en route to a six-part book entitled *Course Correcting – 6 Steps to Getting Your Business On Track for Success!* Not that there are only six steps; just that I've found six to be key to navigating this route and learned many lessons in the process.

In the process of navigating this route multiple times, I've also come across questions, comments, criticisms and objections, as well as answer, which I posed to a group of people who have successfully made this trek in one form or another to get their thoughts. I framed these comments to this Delphi Group in advance in the form of Question Sets by topic, which I will share with you in the next section. You may resonate with them, you might scoff at them but I did not make them up. I've heard every one of these in real life. We then completed recorded interviews that yielded a rich base of understanding which I've drawn upon in shaping this book.

That knowledge base was augmented by a significant amount of research into the extensive knowledge base you can find online if you search with a purpose. That information usually confirmed what I had heard but sometimes it differed. I've hyperlinked all of it so that you can see for yourself and reach a conclusion that is right for you.

Which brings us to the topic of this book – *Crafting an Operating Strategy that Fits You!*

You can read this book offline and it will tell you a lot. You can read online and selectively probe deeper by hyperlinking to the extensive resource base to which it lead you. You can find articles, blogs, book reviews, websites, even books themselves upon which you can build quite a knowledge base. The entire structure of the book is purposely designed to enable you to leverage the power of the Internet to become very knowledgeable about the issues involved in creating an effective business strategy. Not just checklist-deep; *knowledgeable!*

But knowledge is useless unless you apply it. This book is intended to give you the tools you'll need but it will up to you to apply them in order to achieve the success you have in mind.

Please join me on our common journey....

Introduction

Over the last few decades, I've repeatedly found myself in the position of being a change agent.

I hate to tell you but the human animal does not like change.

If you are trying to start up a company, turnaround a company or transform a company or some subset of one, you are by definition *leading change*.

When I've worked with people to craft a strategy by which to accomplish a goal that required doing anything differently than letting inertia take its course, here is what I heard:

- We know what we're good at. We just need to do more of it.
- We're not a solution, we're a component.
- My strategy is to increase sales. What else?
- Why plan when you know things will change before the plan's done?
- Don't waste time planning; just get something in front of customers.
- Let's wait and see how things turn out. We can plan then.
- My business model is simple. I sell it, you buy it.
- My mission is to make money. Why do I need a statement for that?
- What is this Culture garbage? People come here to work.
- We hire for Cultural fit first, competence second. We can always train them.
- That model wouldn't fit our culture and you can't change a culture.
- Forget strategy; focus on culture. A strong culture eats strategy for lunch.
- Writing a business plan is too time-consuming. Let's just do a P&L and be done.
- It's impossible to plan for all the eventualities. We'll figure it out when it happens.
- We don't have the people to write a plan. We can't get that done and still get this product to market in time for the big show.

You can find many books which deal with big strategy issues; I've given you links to several of them. But few if any deal with all the issues involved in bringing theory to practice while addressing the uniqueness's of *your* business, *your* culture, *your* goal.

If *you* are now in the hot seat, join me on a journey I've taken many times and let me help you deal with these issues as you *Craft an Operating Strategy that Fits You!*

Crafting an Operating Strategy That Fits You!

The adrenaline is flowing within you!

You've envisioned a business success that you're burning to create and crystallized an outcome that you want to achieve! It's like seeing an island on the horizon when you're adrift at sea. You know where you want to go but you ask "how do you get from here to there in spite of all the funny things lurking everywhere," paraphrasing Dr. Seuss.

A vision without a plan is like that island, a tantalizing dream, until you can define how to turn it into reality. That's the essence of crafting a strategy.

Let's start by adding substance to your vision…

Shape your Vision - The 3 P's of "Good to Great"

In his seminal book, _Good to Great_, Jim Collins serves a smorgasbord of prerequisites to business greatness which he derived from his teams' many years of consulting experience at McKinsey & Co. Leaders aspiring to build great organizations still turn to Jim Collins' teachings to answer the many questions that confront them along the way.

Among his many lessons, his message in Chapter 5 stands out as a guidepost for anyone trying to navigate the inevitable forks in the road to greatness.

Jim calls this chapter "The Hedgehog Concept."

The what? As wise as his message, people can find its title arcane, the chapter can seem byzantine to read and it is even more challenging to summarize so it is difficult to share and apply its important message even though it really helps you cut through the confusion of conflicting options to get to an answer that will weather the tests to come.

Experienced leaders know they need a simple mnemonic when presenting big ideas to others, preferably following the rule of "three."

So how can one convey "The Hedgehog Concept" in three words?

Answer: The 3 P's.

If you are seeking the right path forward but need a guideline that is:

> ➢ easy-to-remember,
> ➢ easy-to-apply,
> ➢ easy-to-present,

you'll see when you read Jim's chapter that it translates into the 3 P's of:

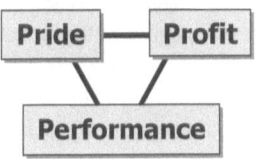

- **Pride**

  This can also be called Passion but we're talking business and it's not enough to love what you do. You and your team need to feel a sense of *pride* in what you're doing in order to subliminally communicate its value to those around you, whether colleagues or customers, and to keep everyone fueled when the going gets tough.

- **Profit**

  Any endeavor needs a source of funding in order to operate and thereby continue to provide that source of pride. In business, we call this "Profit." The concept is just as relevant in *pro bono* charities, not-for-profit NGO's and medical, military and public safety operations. Simply put, the endeavor must be able to sustain itself.

- **Performance**

  The endeavor needs to be the "Best" in *its* world at what it does. Best can be defined in many ways but if the endeavor can't stand above the herd of competitors and alternatives who will try to eat its lunch, it won't thrive, much less serve as a source of pride.

Imagine a three-legged stool. Take out one of its legs and the stool will fall. Similarly, you can see that the absence of any one of these three attributes will undermine the survival of the whole. The presence of all three will virtually *guarantee* its success!

Leaders taking the reins of a multi-product, multi-market business can quickly find the rich field of dreams they inherited has become a quagmire of questions that will devour them in the absence of a simple benchmark against which to judge all the options.

So too, for anyone planning a greenfield venture. There are always more opportunities than resources to address them. So how do you pick the one that will succeed?

Use the 3 P's as your test. The "3 P's" apply whether you're planning a product, shaping a business or evaluating a potential job opportunity. They can even provide a useful tool for counseling people as they build their career!

I've used this "three-legged stool" as a communications tool for over two decades in transforming a global electronics company, creating a hot pre-IPO venture, turning around restarts and counseling clients. NO one has ever not "gotten it' instantly!

Try this succinct yet fundamental decision-making tool the next time *you* find "two roads diverging in a wood" as you're shaping your vision for the future.

Pride, Profit, Performance!

Define your Vision as a Solution

Mike Bosworth, Author of <u>Solution Selling,</u> makes it crystal clear: "No pain, no change."

Mike is talking about the inertia which keeps people in their *status quo* even though they know they would benefit from making a change. This is not a business phenomenon, this is a human trait. <u>Dr. Kelly Weselman</u> is an Atlanta-area physician treating patients with chronic conditions whose symptoms would be alleviated were they to lose weight. She makes a weight-loss recommendation many times each day, which the patients acknowledge, then ignore. Without prompting for the answer I knew would come, I asked her, "What does it take to get a patient to lose weight?" Her answer?

"Their first heart attack!"

The pain of maintaining the *status quo* has to be worse than the challenge of changing it in order to overcome the preference for "the devil you know versus the devil you don't."

The world has existed without you for a long time so why would anyone change what they're doing now if there is nothing *dramatic* to be gained from that change? Any change involves risk to the *status quo* so your "solution" can't be just a "nice to have."

The "pain" associated with that *status quo* must be severe enough to bring it to the top of the stack of issues competing for attention. Until it's there, it doesn't matter how good your "solution" is because it's not doing anything. Once the pain is at the top of the stack, your Vision must be perceived as *the Best Solution* to the issue behind that pain.

So before you go any further, ask yourself three questions:

- **What is the pain you solve?**
- **Who do you solve it for?**
- **How do you solve it in a differentiated way?**

You *must* be able to answer these three questions! You might know everything there is to know about *what* you propose to do but if doing it won't solve a pain for a specific group of people that you can define and do so in a way that is differentiated from their available alternatives, you won't provide a credible solution to a market through which you can build business value.

Plus you won't be able to raise the money to do it. Here's an OpenView blog on the topic, where the same questions are posed but in a different order (I believe you need to know the answer to **Who** before you can define **How** the **What** is differentiated.)

Same message: Define your Vision as a Solution.

If this message is too theoretical, let's take a look at the practical.

Brian Tracy appeared on The Dan Vega Show with this blunt message:

"The single most important ingredient for business success is that you have an excellent product or service to begin with and that you are constantly looking for ways to make that product or service better for your customers.

"If that is the central focus of your business, then you are going to be successful. If that is *not* the central focus of your business, then you will not be."

His statement crisply captures the importance of manifesting your vision in a form that solves a real need for paying customers.

- ✓ *Customers that have a pain which you can solve.*
- ✓ *Customers that you can efficiently target.*
- ✓ *Customers that will view you as their Best Choice.*

So how will you accomplish that objective?

Plan a Route to your Vision

The more cynical among us will tell you that a Plan only exists to give you something to change! Others will go so far as to say "Don't Plan, Just Sell!"

Do you really *need* a Business Plan?

This question even gets serious discussion in this Entrepreneur magazine article.

The dilemma is that business environments change so fast that it will seem that any comprehensive plan has become obsolete by the time it gets printed. Conversely, if the elements of vision, strategy and path to liquidity aren't formulated into a systematic plan of action, chaos will soon reign and make it impossible to keep a team on task. Plus, the first thing an investor, Board member or bank officer will ask for is "The Plan."

The Plan! Perhaps that phrase seems daunting, perhaps it constrains your vision or perhaps you are already opening up an Excel worksheet ready to crunch numbers!

Before you do any of that, ask yourself, "Where does the money flow?" The answer may seem obvious: You build a product and then you sell it to someone who pays you for it.

Really? Look at a magazine. People write articles that get published in the magazine. Are those articles the product? Is the magazine even the product? It gets sold to subscribers (sometimes); doesn't that make them the customers? Actually, they are the *product*! Advertisers pay a lot of money to publishers for the privilege of putting ads for *their* products in front of those subscribers.

Subscription fees merely underwrite the cost of documenting the number of subscribers the magazine produces. It's the flow of advertising dollars that is the source of profit for the magazine so the advertisers are the customers. The content is merely the honey that attracts the subscribers.

This business model is typical for any media business but is irrelevant to a manufacturer selling products that have a high variable cost. Getting *your* business model right is crucial! Think about the optimal flow of money for your business before you start building a P&L statement.

- Should you sell a product? Deliver a service? Give it away for free in order to yield revenue from someone who wants access to your "customer"?
- Should you sell to your users directly or through an intermediary?
- Do you want a one-time payment or an annuity revenue stream? Are your costs front-loaded or back-ended?

All of these questions and more will shape your optimum business model and it's something you *cannot* easily change later. I've seen people try and it can be disastrous.

Think you can sell a product up front and promise to deliver free user services thereafter? What happens to cash flow when new product sales dry up? I've seen this.

Think you can sell through distribution and then try to go direct to the same market? What happens when your resellers bolt to a competing supplier? I've seen this.

Think you can turn an enterprise software vendor into a SaaS provider? What happens when next-quarter revenues suddenly dry up as a result? I've seen this.

Get your business model *right* from the start!

You're crafting a strategy to create or transform a business but hold off on building a Business *Plan* until you've defined a Business *Model* that works!

This discussion from OpenView Labs confirms the importance of qualifying key structural elements of your business before you even begin building your business model! It points you to several experts on the topic, including Tom Eisenmann, a professor at Harvard Business School, who has built a "20-Questions" table you might find to be a helpful tool along with a comprehensive discussion of key business model questions to answer at VentureFizz.

Steve Blank, a Silicon Valley success story, points out that "a business model describes how your company creates, delivers and captures value." The essence of a business is creating value so building a model of how that value gets captured is crucial.

Steve goes on to emphasize the importance of building a dynamic model before freezing it into a static plan. Why "dynamic"? Because it will likely take several iterations to get it to a "repeatable and scalable" form! Check out the hyperlink. You'll find other helpful resources there as well.

Steven Koltai, a very successful entrepreneur, executive and Brookings Institution Visiting Scholar, takes the topic a step further by pointing out that building *multiple* revenue streams into your model will make it more robust!

Drawing on his experience running strategy for Warner Bros. and teaching "Popcorn," a popular course at the USC School of Film and Television, he described how the movie industry makes itself more resilient by tapping into at least *four* separate revenue streams in film distribution. The resulting model is less vulnerable to weakness in any one stream, it offers more opportunities to find "under the radar" revenue that can make your business more profitable than your competitor's and you can add ancillary revenues to your primary source to create a blend of upfront and recurring cash flows.

This choice of what cash you tap into and how you tap into it is the essence of defining your "Business Model," a *prerequisite* to building "The Plan."

So first, determine who has a need which you can resolve that will create a result for which *someone* will pay money.

The person with the need which you intend to resolve may *not* be the one who will pay the money to get the result. Maybe someone else will pay to get a result of the result. Perhaps the need is valid but no one is willing to pay enough to fund the result.

Before you begin paving the path to liquidity, ensure you know how the gold will flow!

Then, articulate your pitch. No spreadsheets. Yet! Just a simple, one-sentence pitch that you can deliver with pride and for which you have the conviction that you can perform! *(Remember the 3 P's.)*

"Hello, my name / company is _____.
Identify who you are

I / We help _____

Identify the segment with the need

_____

*Verb phrase describing what you enable **them** to do, to have or to become*

So that _____.

Describe the beneficial result they will obtain from your capability

Say this phrase to a spouse, a friend, a business partner, a few times. Do you believe it? Do they "buy it?" Do you feel good about what you are promising to do?

If so, you not only have your pitch down, you have defined your Mission!

This simple Mission Statement becomes the foundation around which you can build a winning business. Now, let's take a look at the Values your business will need to embody in order to fulfill this Mission.

Unless you've invented wearable anti-gravity, someone else is already satisfying the need you've targeted, maybe not as well, maybe not as reliably, maybe not as inexpensively, but they're out there or soon will be.

They and all their competitors will make competing sales claims. What is it you will *stand for* that will set you apart?

Will you be the Highest Quality, Lowest Cost, Best Value, First (which doesn't even guarantee your survival!), Only (which only lasts until someone else enters your market), Fastest to Respond, Best Customer Service, The Premier Provider?

The Values that are Key to your Mission are Key to your Culture.

That which sets you apart defines the Values that must be reflected in your Culture. You can't stand for something you don't represent, you can't stand for nothing and still be something, and you can't be all things to all people.

Align your Strategy and your Culture

Your path to liquidity (See Chapter 1) governs a lot about how you can operate. Company culture also governs a lot about how you can operate. A successful operating strategy must take both of these constraints into account.

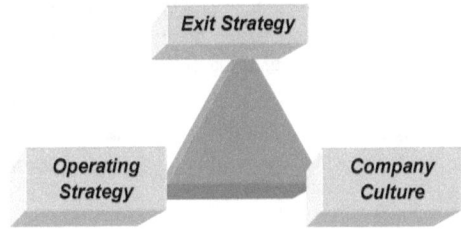

If the apparent "best operating strategy" conflicts with one of these constraints, then either that constraint or the strategy needs to change. Better to reconcile disconnects now than to self-destruct later!

It's a lot more difficult to change a culture than it is to change a strategy. Depending on the available runway and the degree to which the existing culture is embedded, it may be more practical to develop a strategy that is consistent with the existing culture, even if it is not the strategy with the highest potential payoff. An established organization inherently wants to maintain "homeostasis", that state in which the myriad forces within the organization are at equilibrium. Disrupting that equilibrium will be met with internal resistance, whether it is overt rebellion or passive-aggressive apathy. If the culture can't easily be changed in an affordable timeframe, a sub-optimal strategy could yield better near-term results than a great strategy that gets torpedoed by internal politics.

But what if those results aren't going to be good enough?

Then you start with the optimal strategy and change the culture to match it.

What? Change the Culture? Didn't Peter Drucker say "Culture Eats Strategy for Lunch?"

Aside from the argument over whether he actually said those words, in order for it to be effective, the Strategy needs to be reinforced by the Culture. In order to mold the Culture to fit the Strategy, the essential Values underpinning that Strategy *must* be defined and then succinctly and consistently communicated to the people. It may be necessary to bring in new people who naturally espouse that Culture and to move out people who notably reject that Culture. I've found that it takes about 35% of the people overtly embodying a Culture that a charismatic leader publicly espouses to shift the attitudes of another 55% of the people to at least go along with the values called for by that Culture. 10% of the people will rigidly adhere to the old culture and they need to quickly find new homes in order for the 55% to not look back at the "good old days."

And it doesn't happen overnight. You need enough financial runway to see a cultural change through, which is why "companies with a chronic shortage of funds can be trapped by an entrenched culture" as Chuck Auster pointed out to me.

The argument over which comes first, Culture or Strategy, continues. Check the three preceding embedded links for some interesting points of view on the topic and if you want to read a success story about changing the culture of a large organization, try Lou Gerstner's epic about changing IBM, *Who Says Elephants Can't Dance?*

If that's too epic for you, Chuck Auster's friend David Shaner has written a book on and devotes his website to the topic of *The Seven Arts of Change*. Click the link and watch the slide show at the top right of his home page as it scrolls through The Seven Arts. As they unfold, they bring instant understanding of the depths of thinking it takes to go beyond sloganeering to get to where you can yield "business transformation that lasts."

Let's take this a step further. If you *can* change a culture, what are the attributes of a culture that you would want to imbue in your business?

For an answer to this question, I turned to Dr. Vlatka Hlupic, Professor of Business and Management at the Westminster Business School of the University of Westminster in London, a former Adjunct Faculty member at the London Business School, the CEO of the Drucker Society London and a renowned Leadership and Change Management consultant. In her book, The Management Shift, to be published by Palgrave Macmillan in November 2014, she advances a 5-Level Emergent Leadership Model in which she postulates that a dramatic expansion in productivity occurs when a company transitions from a Level 3 leadership model to a Level 4 leadership model.

EMERGENT LEADERSHIP

	INDIVIDUAL	ORGANISATIONAL
Level 5	Limitless	Unbounded
Level 4	Enthusiastic	Collaborative
Level 3	Controlled	Orderly
Level 2	Reluctant	Stagnating
Level 1	Lifeless	Apathetic

Reprinted from "The Management Shift - How to Harness the Power of People and Transform Your Organization for Sustainable Success" by Dr. Vlatka Hlupic. Published by Palgrave Macmillan, November 2014.

Dr. Hlupic has studied the cultural dynamics of organizations for years and has found that Level 3 typifies the cultural norm, 50% of companies in her view, where "orderliness" is the governing dynamic by which the employee base operates within well-defined limits following well-defined procedures. Safety and compliance requirements may force the organization to encourage this culture and many employees will feel very comfortable operating in an environment where their responsibilities and duties are so well-defined. In my own experience, some of these people will be loyal and committed while others are merely "going through the motions" since there is a limit to how engaged they can become emotionally without risking going "outside the box."

Once such a culture has become established, the people within it can cling to the clarity it offers but Dr. Hlupic finds they do not feel passionate about their work. Homeostasis preserves this culture, which can serve a useful purpose when compliance, security, consistency and quality control are crucial. Think of airline operations, health care test labs, financial institutions, etc. But a "control" culture is not conducive to innovation.

For a perfect illustration of a Level 3 culture, here's a quote excerpted from a Harvard Business Review blog by Ron Ashkenas (Managing Partner of Schaffer Consulting) and Lisa Bodell (Founder and CEO of FutureThink), wherein they discuss the causes behind the conundrum that many organizations promote innovation that they don't condone:

"...the reality in many organizations today is that despite the public emphasis on innovation, the underlying culture may be strongly risk-averse. As one senior manager in a large financial institution said to one of us, "The key to success here is to never make the same mistake once."

Even worse, Dr. Hlupic believes that as many as 10-25% of organizations operate in a Level 2 environment of reluctant stagnation, missing out on opportunities that would be available to them had they a more engaged employee base and vibrant climate.

In contrast, shifting the leadership style upward to Level 4 unleashes a higher level of employee engagement in which the desired attributes are Passion, Innovation, Empowerment, even Autonomy! *But* with that engagement comes risk.

Making this Shift requires a higher level of enthusiasm for their work on the part of the people and a climate of collaboration and tolerance for risk within the organization. Dr. Hlupic describes the dynamics of this shift in Chapter 4 of her book, "The Emerging Leadership Model – From the Stagnating to the Unbounded Culture."

The Key to making this Shift? It must start from the Top!

An inspirational leadership team must actively espouse the attributes of a Level 4 culture and moreover, embody them. "Walking the Talk" begets a "ripple effect" which spreads throughout the organization, building back up from the bottom in the same way a wave reinforces itself from the shore.

This "rebound from the bottom" is essential to this new culture taking hold in those functional units in which it can positively impact the organization.

But management has to set the pace and that means risking the *disorderliness* inherent in an environment where the employee base, naturally comprising a larger proportion of the people within the organization than management, feels empowered, passionate, even autonomous. Making this shift can call for a lot of courage at the top!

Ashkenas and Bodell go on to say in their [blog], "successful innovation does indeed require a tolerance for risk-taking and learning from periodic failure." The implication of these two phrases is that management has to tolerate not just the risk but failure itself!

Looking up to Level 5 gets even scarier! Individuals without limits, organizations without bounds? Sounds like anarchy to me!

I broached that concern to Professor Hlupic and what ensued was a fascinating journey to what in concept could be the Model Organization.

The first step was her admission that Level 5 couldn't normally apply to an entire company; it was a team-level, time-limited goal-focused construct.

A "skunk works!" I described to her Lockheed's Skunk Works where Kelly Johnson developed the SR-71 Blackbird, the hypersonic reconnaissance aircraft that flew above the stratosphere. A clandestine team operating in the desert outside the constraints of a giant corporation totally focused on going outside the box to develop the impossible. Once they succeeded, the team essentially disbanded.

"Yes," she agreed, "that is a good example."

So, Level 5 exists as an extension of a Level 4 organization, breaking through barriers while the core organization operates within them. I characterized the motivations of the Level 5 inhabitants as Self-Actualizing per Abraham Maslow's "Hierarchy of Needs", an observation with which she enthusiastically agreed.

In fact, she went on to equate the motivations within Level 4 to Maslow's Esteem level. We were on a roll!

"What about Level 3?" I asked. Isn't there a place for it as well? "Yes," Dr. Hlupic acknowledged. That is where Maslow's "Belonging" motivation rules and "it can be a necessary level within an organization." Think of those components that must ensure compliance, security, safety, process consistency, test accuracy, etc. It can be difficult to generate enthusiasm for doing the same thing over and over but it can be necessary that constancy and commitment trump enthusiasm.

No organization benefits from the Reluctance and Stagnation of Level 2 (not to mention the Apathy of Level 1 "other than for prisons", per Dr. Hlupic) yet Dr. Hlupic finds a whopping 10-25% of companies nevertheless linger in the Purgatory of Level 2.

So in theory, an ideal organization could comprise a blend of Levels 3, 4 and 5 with the revenue drivers of the organization operating in Level 4. Functional units such as sales, marketing, recruiting, product development, business development, customer service, corporate strategy, engineering, even production. Places where enthusiasm, innovation and operating freedom enable the organization to nimbly serve its marketplace.

Supporting those outward-facing units are the units charged with ensuring the trains run on time. Places such as scheduling, security, compliance auditing, accounting, QA, air traffic control, maintenance, order processing, etc., which can benefit from the order, control and consistency of Level 3.

But we can't stay where we are forever or someone will catch up with us! We *need* those free-thinkers, those barrier-breakers. Places like R&D, new venture incubators, skunk works. The Self-Actualizers of Level 5. Places where it is okay to fail, just not okay to give up.

In this model, we're not trying to shift the entire organization from Level 3 to Level 4. We're building an organization *led* from Level 4, supported where needed on Level 3 and aspiring to what Level 5 can deliver.

A organization that spans the top three levels of the Emergent Leadership Model while it climbs out of Level 2 and any remnants of Level 1, to which I'd add the Level 0 of those who would rebel at any of this.

The key to making this multi-level model work is a shift in the culture of the *management team* from Level 3 to Level 4. You can't lead from Level 3 and be able to espouse, much less tolerate, the freedoms of Level 4. Dr. Hlupic confirms that when people with Level 4 attributes find themselves reporting to Level 3 leaders, they often complain of feeling "micromanaged." Moreover, the organization itself can become stifled since it is being managed to orderliness rather than to innovation.

Dr. Hlupic views my inclusion of Level 3 within this ideal model with caution as she sees unleashing the passion of *all* players as bringing great exuberance to the organization. I come at it from extensive experience operating in hazardous environments where the adherence to procedures of Level 3 keeps people alive. The leadership challenge lies in effectively bridging the passion of Level 4 with the orderliness of Level 3.

The same holds true in dealing with Level 5. It is necessary to risk failure if you are to break through boundaries but the impact of such a failure can't jeopardize the survival of the organization as a whole. The leadership challenge lies in containing the risk.

An example is the crash of Virgin Galactic's SpaceShipTwo. Virgin Galactic is pioneering manned commercial space flight, a high-risk endeavor if there ever was one! The crash is a set-back for Virgin Galactic, one with which they are prepared to cope, but it is a virtual non-event for the other companies comprising the Virgin Group.

So in aligning our strategy and our culture, we must look first at ourselves as leaders! Do we have what it takes to lead from Level 4? If not, that might define the best strategy for our business as one grounded in Level 3. Or, it might mean we need to bring on Level 4 leadership and trust them with it.

Are we operating at Level 5? That's great when we're breaking barriers to create a business but that unbounded culture can't continue to dominate as we get traction and start to grow an operating company.

As Chuck Auster commented, there is a point at which the Level 5 Entrepreneur has to morph into the Level 4 Leader or else turn over the reins to someone who is. David Campbell comes at it from the opposite direction, pointing out that there is more to effective Leadership than the controlled management skills epitomized by Level 3.

As we create our growth Strategy, we need to anticipate the *changes* in Culture that must transpire as we expand, as well as the need to allow the different cultures appropriate to different functions to co-exist within the overall dynamic of an enthusiastic, collaborative Level 4-dominant enterprise.

The symmetry of Dr. Hlupic's Emergent Leadership Model with Maslow's Hierarchy of Needs leaps out at you, suggesting that the operating psychology of the organizational units and the motivational needs of their inhabitants need to be in sync for the organization to reach its full potential.

This does *not* mean that the operating psychology and motivational needs must be uniform throughout the organization. Far from it! What it illustrates is that the style needs to match the mission of the organizational *unit*. The Emergent Leadership Model really tells me that one Culture does *not* fit all within an operationally-integrated organization!

I'll go a step further and say that Dr. Hlupic's 5-Level Model is particularly useful in portraying the range of cultures and motivational needs that can be encountered across a large organization. The truly effective leader in such an organization is comfortable, or at least competent, in working across the top *three* levels in order to be in tune with their disparate needs. This need to stretch up or down levels makes an even stronger case for well-grounded Level 4 leadership at the core of an organization's management team. It also provides a glimpse into their management future for leaders of young companies aspiring to acquire, get acquired or go public.

One human attribute that *does* offer a common ground from Level 3 to Level 5 is the need people have for a sense of purpose in their lives. People who find a sense of purpose in their work become highly engaged in that work, even passionate about it!

It doesn't matter whether they are Self-Actualizing in a Skunk Works, seeking Esteem in Level 4 or Belonging within an orderly, repetitive Level 3 process. The feeling that what they're doing matters to an outcome in which they believe gives them a sense of purpose that bonds them to the organization. The effective leader *ensures* that a sense of purpose pervades the organization and in that effort, espouses the core of Level 4.

Cornelia Shipley, an executive coach and human capital specialist, makes the point that with a common sense of purpose comes the need to integrate your strategy across *all* your business sectors to avoid the creation of silo's and to leverage the scale advantages of the robust organization you will have created.

Dr. Hlupic's belief that 10-25% of organizations are operating at Level 2 of the Model additionally points out the value that could be extracted were Level 4 management to unlock the energy bottled up within these Level 2 organizations. Rather than expecting management laggards to evolve upward, the Model suggests that Level 2 companies represent targets of opportunity for Level 4 teams to complement their organic growth strategy with an inorganic strategy aimed at harvesting this latent energy.

Viewed in this way, the 5-Level Emergent Leadership Model offers *three* important insights: (a) it provides a behavioral map of the range of an organization's operating needs correlated with the motivational needs of its corresponding people, (b) it promises that a productivity increase can be unleashed by evolving to a Level 4 leadership and dominant operating culture and (c) it points to a strategic opportunity to accelerate an organization's growth by capitalizing on the value locked up in Level 2 competitors.

Dr. Hlupic cautions, however, that levels cannot be skipped in the process of executing a "management shift", saying "One cannot go from Level 2 to Level 4 without spending some time at Level 3." Her comment provides an important insight into the dynamics of achieving The Management Shift which would need to be taken into account when transitioning companies or functional units to higher levels. Just as Maslow's Hierarchy of Needs describes a progression so too does the Emergent Leadership Model describe hierarchical levels of enlightenment wherein the motivational needs of the people and the norms of their function's culture would need to be *progressively* evolved upward.

To help organizations (and their leaders) identify their dominant culture and begin The Management Shift upward, Dr. Hlupic turns to a diagnostic tool she has developed called the 6 Box Leadership Model as described in her book, which she has used in 20 organizations worldwide to help them progressively navigate the passage to Level 4.

Ashkenas and Bodell also offer four helpful tips to promoting an innovation mindset in their HBR blog, one of which is to "Use the right words to encourage the right culture."

With all this shifting amid Cultures that might vary across the organization, are there any constants? Absolutely!

The Values for which the organization stands are its bedrock.

Going back to an earlier statement in this chapter:

The Values that are Key to your Mission are Key to your Culture.

First, the Mission, then the Values, then the Culture.

Jim Collins starts even further back in *Good to Great,* saying "First Who, then What." My friend Jim Furneaux made that point up front in our discussion: "Know yourself first." He advises "Look at your skill set; don't jump into dark water. Find skilled people with a passion for the model," citing Bright Horizons as a business that was born directly from the emotional synergies of Bessemer Ventures and Bain & Co.

If you're building a business within a larger organization, "Know yourself" can extend to being realistic about the constraints within which you can operate there. Conversely, you might find that to be successful, the business has to be moved outside those constraints, witness the successes of the "PayPal Mafia."

Sometimes the Who defines the Values, the Values beget the Culture and the Culture becomes its own source of strength, not to be tinkered with for the sake of a Strategy. Such a viewpoint underlies the success behind Tom Miller's company, T. R. Miller & Co. In a long conversation with Tom, I was beyond impressed with how much his own values have shaped a company he started 38 years ago and has since crafted into a sustained success!

Opportunities he has foregone because they conflicted with those values. Acquisitions he hasn't made because they would have made him too big for his company's culture to survive. Tom also advises "Keep your ambitions in check." He cites a friend who over-extended himself and crashed his company because he let his ego outrun his resources, hence Tom's reluctance to grow merely for the sake of growth.

We'll talk more about Tom in Chapter 6, "Getting to Best in Your Business" but the message here is that he came to his business with a solid set of core values and has succeeded because he stayed true to himself while he focused on serving others. What a Strategy!

So what about the question of whether to hire for Culture or Competence?

People with the Competence to perform their roles within this multi-level cultural model will likely align with the best Culture for their function by self-selection. What if they don't? "Misfits can sap the energy out of any Culture regardless of their Competence", cautions Dr. Hlupic.

Conversely, "Culture *may* eat Strategy for lunch", per Peter Drucker (maybe) but it can't come without Competence. Ultimately, you need to find or train competent people whose motivational needs fit the *needed* Culture for their mission, which is not necessarily the culture you have now.

However, time can be a deadly enemy. Jim Furneaux points out "You don't have time to *build* competence in a short-window business" so Strategy, Culture and Competence become a tightly-coupled recursive loop.

This may suggest a limit to the span of cultural Levels which can exist in an enterprise starved for either or both of cash and time. Scott Maxwell, Founder & Senior Managing Director of OpenView Venture Partners, suggests there is a bound on the cultural variance that can be sustained across an organization without risking fragmentation, preferring instead to outsource functions whose needed culture doesn't match the mainstream.

Scott referenced John Sculley's book "Odyssey" as predicting the rise of outsourcing, a concept famously reprised by Geoff Moore in the phrase "core versus context", drawn from his book *Dealing with Darwin* and discussed in this Inc.com interview. It is often easier to manage suppliers than to manage employees and outsourcing non-core functions allows management to focus on that which defines the company and underlies its competitive advantage.

What about the trend toward creating a "happy place" at work as a means of motivating people to perform at a higher level?

A recent Fast Company magazine article by Mark Crowley, *Why Being Engaged At Work Isn't As Simple As "Being Happy",* shreds this approach!

He cites a discussion with Jim Clifton, the CEO of Gallup Research for the past 26 years, in which Clifton told him emphatically "The idea of trying to make people happy at work is terrible."

Gallup's research shows that how a person *feels about the work they do* every day has the greatest impact on engagement by far.

"What companies will inevitably find is the only way to make a person happy is to give them a job that matches well to their strengths, a boss who cares about their development and a mission that gives them feelings of purpose."

Gallup's findings about engagement "are really about a human wanting to develop, maximize their strengths, make a meaningful contribution, and feel valued. And we know that engagement happens automatically when these deeper needs get met."

When Clifton was asked where organizations should start if their objective is to build deep and lasting engagement across their enterprises, he was direct and unambiguous.

"Going forward, we must insist on hiring caring managers. Managers must be driven, love productivity, profitability, and competing," he added, "but they must also have an inclination to maximize the potential of every person on their team."

Gallup's research shows that unimaginable success results when companies demonstrate greater discipline--and courage--by selecting people who have the proven motivation of making a difference in the lives of others, not just their own.

"The final question companies should ask each time they're considering a managerial candidate is this: Do they *offer* leadership or do they *need* leadership? It's a big difference," Clifton says.

A difference that directly underscores Dr. Hlupic's belief in the importance of The Management Shift!

Whether you decide to take the expeditious approach of aligning your strategy to fit the existing culture or the more ambitious approach of adopting a strategy and then evolving your culture to align it with the strategy, you must ensure the operating strategy and the culture are aligned and that together, they support your path to liquidity!

(By the way, if you're still into "perks at work" people-pleasing, check out this New York Times article, *The Downsides of Generous Workplace Perks!*)

Capture all this in a simple Business Plan

Okay, we're down to the short straw: writing down what it is you plan to do!

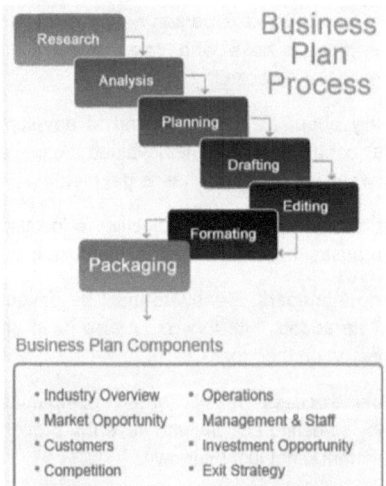

"Planning is an unnatural process; it is much more fun to do something. The nicest thing about not planning is that failure comes as a complete surprise!"

Ground Floor Partners

Business plan writers and consultants

www.groundfloorpartners.com

Washington State University has created a large but clever infographic depicting the planning process for a business for which there is a more detailed discussion on *Investopedia* ("Four Steps to Creating a Stellar Business Plan") describing the rationale for the various elements called for in a business plan.

You can find the richest resource at the Small Business Administration, *How to Write a Business Plan*. You must be a private company with no more than 50 employees to get a loan from the SBA but anyone can benefit from the information on their website!

If you don't have the time, the discipline or the interest to do this work, the good news is there are people who will do it for you!

Check out Ground Floor Partners, mentioned above or BPlanExperts at http://bplanexperts.com/ for two examples. Here's an article BPlanExperts published in 2013 making the case for a structured approach to planning:

"**Business Planning: A structured approach** - A majority of entrepreneurs accept the need for creating a business plan however, a few often fail to realize that an effective and comprehensive business plan can lay down a road map to success for their businesses.

While a professionally crafted business plans does not guarantee success, for entrepreneurs with great business ideas, it certainly increases the probability of them crossing the finishing line sensationally.

Often a business plan is used as a sales document with an aim to impress an investor, rather than provide an extensive strategic and operational road map of the venture. This often fails to achieve the desired results, leading to entrepreneurs blaming the vehicle i.e. the usefulness of a business plan rather than the quality of goods being transported, i.e. the content included in the document. A business plan needs to capture the essence of a business and its delivery mechanism to attract investments.

At BPlanExperts we believe that without a proper structure, or by using cookie cutter templates a business plan become rudderless with essential information and data ending up in a haphazard and reactive manner, thereby losing its basic intent and purpose.

If drafted professionally, a business plan has the ability to serve multiple activities, as shown below.

• **Maximize on opportunities:** Comprehensive plans help businesses to channelize their finance, resources and most prominently their time in the course of success. Capitalization of a business idea can improved with the creation of a well crafted strategic business plan which distinctly demonstrates the true value of a business idea. Simply put, a business plan is the first marketing tool for a business.

• **Focused to the script:** Often entrepreneurs are so fanatical about their business idea that they lose sight of reality during the startup phase of their businesses. As the sea of emotions, doubt, fear and exhaustion clinches, the sight of a business plan helps stick to predefined goals and objectives. A business plan can prevent entrepreneurs from taking wrong decisions in the silhouette of emotions.

• **Look into the future:** Comprehensive business plans acts as a catalyst to help manage entrepreneurial businesses more efficiently and effectively. It assists to put strategic considerations onto a paper and consequently allows stakeholders to get better visibility of the business. A business plan can detail alternate future scenarios and set specific objectives and goals for the short, medium and long term. An understanding of the market and the environment in which the business expects to operation are considerably enriched by a thoroughly researched and analyzed business plan.

- **Secure Funds:** To source money from investors or any other structured agency, it is imperative to have a business plan that outlines the future potential of a business and communicates an entrepreneur's vision in a compelling manner. A formal business plan is the basic requirement for seeking funds, be it debt or equity. Most investors will not even consider a funding request without reading through a business plan that is customized to match their regulatory framework.

- **Operationalizing the business:** Execution is key to a business and thus prioritizing jobs, setting up goals and measuring performance each prove vital for the long term sustainability of a venture. Researching the desired market segment and formulating strategies to deliver products and services through the business planning process will ensure that nothing is left to chance from a business perspective.

- **Commitment towards the business:** Last but not the least it is important for entrepreneurs to show their commitment to investors, partners and allied stakeholders. Drafting a comprehensive business plan portrays a high level of seriousness and solid intentions towards the success of a business. It is the first building block of a potential high rise."

Probably the last thing the enthusiastic progenitor of a new business feels like doing is chaining him-or-herself to a desk to structure a business plan. If that is how *you* feel, you'll get a lot out of the next discussion…

Build Resilience into your Plan

Reprising the question about "Why plan when you know things are going to change?" there's a quote attributed to German Field Marshal von Moltke that says roughly "No battle plan survives first contact with the enemy."

If that's true, what's the point of planning?

Dwight Eisenhower answered it best: *"Plans Are Useless, But Planning Is Indispensable!"* General Eisenhower is credited with planning the massive and incredibly complex invasion of Europe during World War II during which many things went wrong yet the Allies prevailed because so much potential failure was taken into account within the planning process.

Chuck Auster echoes this viewpoint when he advises, "In big companies, you need a plan just to keep everybody on the same page. In smaller companies, you need a plan in order to identify downside scenarios so that when you encounter adversity, you've trained for it."

Now that you have worked through all the elements of *your* plan, take a step back and look at where it might fail when you take it to market. *Something* will go wrong. Count on it. But what?

Look at the assumptions and the dependencies in your plan. What is the confidence level you would attribute to them? What would you do if that particular element didn't work as planned? Where would you be unprepared to respond to such a contingency?

Identify those crisis points and ascertain how a set-back there would impact your plan. If it would have significant impact, build the response into your plan now just in case that crisis occurs! You'll "Be Prepared" (the Boy Scout motto) and you'll stun the VC's or Board Members who will expect to trip you up on just such contingencies as these!

If you identify a crisis to which you would be unable to respond, put in an early-warning system now to give you ample time to divert to a new plan should the crisis loom or at least to minimize the loss you'll incur *if* it occurs.

A pilot planning a long-distance flight always identifies suitable alternate airfields along the route to the destination *before* takeoff. The same approach applies to you. It doesn't mean you don't have confidence that you can reach your destination; it just means you are building in options to yield the best possible outcome in the event things don't go as planned.

Steven Koltai strongly recommends that as you implement your plan, you listen to the market response to it. Don't fixate on the rear-view mirror of your plan. You built that plan around data and assumptions that may have been valid then but the market is real-time. If it is telling you something different now, listen to *it*, not the people telling you what the plan called for. Better to declare failure fast so you can morph the plan and adapt it to what it will take to yield a success. "No one will care later whether you were right in the beginning if you are generating success now" says Steven. Conversely, know when to cut your losses if something is just not working. And get expert advice from someone with no vested interest, an independent third-party who can mentor you without having a "dog in the hunt."

Steven Koltai and Chuck Auster are colleagues on the Board of Advisors for the Entrepreneurial Leadership Program (ELP) at Tufts University and Chuck echoes Steven's guidance to "morph to the need as it changes," even to the point of reinventing the company, guidance that Chuck extends to not-for-profit as well as for-profit entities. "The people who backed your original plan want to see you succeed, not die on the cross of a plan that you could have turned into a success by adapting it to the circumstances."

This quote from Winston Churchill makes the point perfectly:

"Success consists of going from failure to failure without loss of enthusiasm."

Now, go craft an Operating Strategy that fits *You!*

Epilog

The book you've just read will be Chapter 3 of the forthcoming full book entitled:

Course Correcting –
6 Steps to Getting Your Business On Track for Success

Chapter Topics will include:

1. **Knowing when you're *NOT* On Track**

2. **Identifying the Shortest Path to Success**

3. Crafting an Operating Strategy that fits You

    a. *Shape your Vision*
    b. *Define your Vision as a Solution*
    c. *Plan a Route to your Vision*
    d. *Align your Strategy and your Culture*
    e. *Capture all this in a simple Business Plan*
    f. *Build Resilience into your Plan*

4. **Honing your Compelling Value Proposition**

5. **Building Predictability into your Sales Pipeline**

6. **Getting to "Best" in your Business**

    Please watch for it. You can sign up on our website for our Newsletter or check for upcoming titles on Amazon.com.

    And let us hear from you! We'd like your feedback, reviews and referrals.

    Thanks for reading!

Thomas C. Browne
www.GrowthUS.com